G. SCHIRMER
✠ EDITION
of
MASSES AND VESPERS

Grand Mass in C Minor

(K. 427)

for

DOUBLE CHORUS OF MIXED VOICES
AND FOUR SOLO VOICES
WITH PIANO ACCOMPANIMENT

by

Wolfgang Amadeus Mozart

Ed. 2240

G. SCHIRMER, Inc.

DISTRIBUTED BY

HAL•LEONARD
CORPORATION
7777 W. BLUEMOUND RD. P.O. BOX 13819 MILWAUKEE, WI 53213

FOREWORD

By a strange trick of fate Mozart was not to finish either of his most important sacred works, the Grand Mass in C Minor and the Requiem. It was death that cut short the composition of the Requiem, while a whole series of unfavorable circumstances prevented the completion of the Mass. It owes its origin to a promise which Mozart gave to his father that he would write a Grand Mass and perform it at Salzburg when he brought Constanze there as his bride. That he was in earnest may be seen from the following passage from a letter of January 4, 1783: "As for the Mass, it is quite true; indeed, I let the pledge flow from my pen on purpose. I made the promise in my heart of hearts." Hence the C Minor Mass was the first large work that Mozart wrote after his marriage, which took place on August 4, 1782. In what spirit he went to work is shown in the following letter addressed to his father, August 17, 1782: "In writing to you the other day I forgot to say that we [Mozart and Constanze] have always attended mass and gone to confession and taken communion together, and I feel that I never prayed so fervently or confessed and took communion so devoutly as by her side. And it was the same with her." Otto Jahn's assumption that we have in this Mass essentially "a work undertaken only as an exercise" is refuted by the content of this letter.

Through the performances every Sunday at Baron van Swieten's Mozart became more closely acquainted with J. S. Bach and Handel. He arranged five Bach fugues for strings; he reworked the instrumentation of several oratorios by Handel at van Swieten's commission. Consequently there is an unmistakable influence of North German, Protestant art in this Mass. The Credo and the Sanctus remind one of Handel, and in the first movement of the Gloria there is even a note-for-note reminiscence from the Hallelujah Chorus of the *Messiah*. The Benedictus, a quartet, breathes the spirit of Bach; the harsh sweetness and the masterly polyphony lend it a wholly distinctive character, stamping it as unique among Mozart's works. His capacity for assimilation is the more remarkable in the light of the fact that at the same time as he was devoting himself to the seriousness and the strict style of such a work as the C Minor Mass he maintained an active connection with the Italian opera buffa, in the style of which he wrote numerous pieces without surrendering his own originality in the least.

When the young couple arrived in Salzburg in July, 1783, the Kyrie, the Gloria, the Sanctus and Benedictus were finished but the Credo was not completed and the Agnus Dei not yet begun. On August 25th of the same year, the first performance took place and it was in Salzburg, at St. Peter's Church, not in Vienna as is stated in the preface to André's edition of the piano score. After this the work was laid to rest for a hundred years, that is to say until April 3, 1901, on which day it celebrated its resurrection in the Martin Luther Church of Dresden. It is not to be assumed that Mozart contented himself with only a fragmentary work for the Salzburg performance. Probably, as Jahn conjectures, he filled in what was missing with pieces from earlier Masses, of which he had written sixteen. Which pieces these were could not be ascertained despite many painstaking attempts. Nissen's assertion that Mozart had finished the Mass while at Salzburg has turned out to be an error.

On his return to Vienna Mozart was at once overwhelmed with teaching duties and work for his many concerts. No opportunity offered itself for the composition of church works. But at the beginning of 1785 there occurred a circumstance that was to prove fateful for the C Minor Mass. Having been invited to write, in a few weeks' time, an Italian oratorio for a Lenten benefit performance at the Burgtheater, the ever-obliging composer undertook the commission. But being unable to compose a new work in the time allotted, he turned to his Mass and adapted the greater part of it for the oratorio. For better or worse it was given an Italian cantata text, and two new arias were composed for it, together with a cadenza for three soloists that was inserted in the concluding fugue of the Gloria. And thus the oratorio, *Davidde penitente*, an occasional and expedient work was finished. It was performed on the

13th and 17th of March, 1785, and was later published. The fate of the Mass was thereby sealed. It remained forgotten in spite of the fragments published by André in 1840, and the score brought out by Breitkopf and Härtel in the collected edition of Mozart's works.

The completed Sanctus and Benedictus, which had been employed in the oratorio, as well as the incomplete movements of the Credo continued unnoticed.

In none of his works, with the exception of the Requiem, did Mozart again reach, let alone surpass, the lofty seriousness and the deep religious dedication of his Grand Mass in C Minor. The strict manner of composition that prevails almost throughout, the use of five and eight-part choruses, the breadth of the solo movements as well as the treatment of the orchestra raise it infinitely above all his earlier works in this genre and place it beside the great Masses of Bach and Beethoven.

From this conviction sprang the wish to reinstate this lofty work in its true significance. For this it was necessary, first, to restore the original text and, second, to provide movements that the Mass lacked. The question arose as to whether we might complete the Mass as had been done very extensively in the case of the Requiem. After mature consideration we concluded that this could be done. The instrumentation of the movements, for which Mozart left complete sketches, was worked out by us. We filled in the missing parts of the Credo from other church works by Mozart, adding them to the whole. (The Köchel numbers of the works used for this purpose are given in the Table of Contents.) As for the Agnus Dei, following the precedent of the Requiem the opening movement of the Mass, namely the Kyrie, was used. Therewith we have a complete Mass.

To the Mozart Society of Dresden and its idealistic officers goes the honor of having planned and carried out the first performance of it. Above all let me here again thank Ernst Lewicki, its inspired director, who is so conversant with Mozart. Without his initiative and his untiring assistance in choosing the supplementary movements the difficult task would not have been started, much less finished.

The two performances sponsored by the aforesaid society on the 3rd and 5th of April, 1901, with the collaboration of the Römhild church choir of the Martin Luther parish and the soloists Frau Schmitt-Csányi, Fraulein T. Rothauser of the Court Opera in Berlin, Willy Schmitt of Frankfort am Main, who was called in at the last minute, and E. Franck of Dresden, gave proof that the work in this new form does not lack the unity that must be one of the basic conditions of every work of art. We may hope that Mozart's C Minor Mass will make its way from Dresden into the entire world, to the honor of its creator, to the joy and exaltation of his friends and admirers.

ALOIS SCHMITT

Dresden, May, 1901.

TABLE OF CONTENTS

Together with identification of the sources of the movements in Mozart's sacred works.

TABLE OF CONTENTS (*Continued*)

We have throughout followed the original manuscript in realizing the organ part for the Mass from the figured bass for organ as the original manuscript has it.

Any other additions are designated in the score by the letter S.

*The choral portion of the Sanctus, especially the orchestral accompaniment of the Osanna double fugue, demonstrates that Mozart composed these movements for double chorus, not for five and four voices respectively. The original manuscript, owned by the Königliche Bibliothek in Berlin contains, in a sheaf of ten-stave music paper, only the score for winds (2 oboes, 2 bassoons, 2 horns, 2 trumpets, and 3 trombones, together with drums). The scores for the chorus and the strings are lost, and it is highly puzzling that these parts have since been published without further ado as five and four-part choruses. Even André can not have possessed the complete choral parts for the Sanctus and Osanna.

Grand Mass in C minor
(K. 427)

№ 1 Kyrie

W. A. Mozart
Completed by Alois Schmitt

Nº 2 Gloria

№ 3 Laudamus te

NB   The next nine bars (to the ✠) may be omitted.

Nº4 Gratias

Nº 5 Domine (Duet)

Nº 6 Qui tollis

43920

Nº 7 Quoniam (Terzett)

tu so_lus Do_mi_nus, tu so_lus al_

tis_ _si_mus.

tis_ _si_mus.

tis_ _si_mus.

46

43920

Nº 8 Jesu Christe

attacco

Cum sancto spiritu

52

43920

53

43920

Nº 9 Credo

Nº 10 Et incarnatus est

ctus est.

Nº 11 Crucifixus

Nº 12 Et resurrexit

№ 13 Et in Spiritum sanctum

Allegro non troppo

Piano

qui lo - cu - tus est per pro - phe - - - tas,

qui lo - cu - tus est per pro - phe - - - tas,

qui lo - cu - tus est per pro - phe - - - tas,

qui lo - cu - tus est per pro - phe - - - tas,

per pro - phe - - - tas.

per pro - phe - - - tas.

per pro - phe - - - tas.

per pro - phe - - - tas.

attacca

№ 14 Credo in unam sanctam

attacca

№ 15 Et vitam venturi saeculi

№ 16 Sanctus

43920

attacca

Osanna

Nº 17 Benedictus (Soloquartet)

43920

43920

Nº 18 Agnus Dei

43920